ANTON BRUCKNER

SYMPHONY No. 9

D minor/d-Moll/Ré mineur
From/Nach
Anton Bruckner: Sämtliche Werke
Kritische Gesamtausgabe
Band IX

Edited by/Herausgegeben von
Leopold Nowak

D1234214

Ernst Eulenburg Ltd

London · Mainz · Madrid · New York · Paris · Prague · Tokyo · Toronto · Zürich

CONTENTS/INHALT

© 1951 Musikwissenschaftlicher Verlag, Wien
Reprinted by permission of Musikwissenschaftlicher Verlag, Wien
Preface © 1951 Musikwissenschaftlicher Verlag, Wien
English translation © 1995 Ernst Eulenburg Ltd
Preface to the Eulenburg edition © 1995 Musikwissenschaftlicher Verlag, Wien
English translation © 1995 Ernst Eulenburg Ltd

Ernst Eulenburg Ltd
48 Great Marlborough Street
London W1V 2BN

PREFACE/VORWORT

New forces were at work in music at the end of the 19th century, as they were in other creative fields. In Germany, Richard Strauss was writing his first symphonic poems, Hans Pfitzner was embarking on his compositional career with the music to Ibsen's *The Feast at Solhaug* and the young Max Reger was starting to attract attention. In France, Claude Debussy was developing Impressionism, and a new world of sound was beginning to open up, influenced by exotic melodies and scales. Gustav Mahler was writing his first three symphonies, while in Italy the *verismo* of Mascagni and Leoncavallo was bringing new orchestral colours into opera, in a style that would soon reach its apogee in the music of Puccini.

It was during these years that Anton Bruckner composed his Ninth Symphony, his unfinished musical testament. The writing of the symphony occupied him from 1887 to 1896. The work stands out from the other music of the time like a being from another world, and half a century later we can see very readily why its great force and prevailing metaphysical tone – the composer dedicated it to 'dem lieben Gott' – were not immediately or fully understood. It was Bruckner's last composition, his *summa musices*, bringing together all of the features that had characterized his symphonic writing: his technique of thematic working, embracing the minutest detail; the creation of thematic groups and interlinking material; the use of contrapuntal elements; the great chorale-like climaxes; and, above all, his power of invention. The sketches for the work show that the Finale was to include both a fugue and an extended chorale.

Ende des 19. Jahrhunderts waren in der Musik wie auf anderen Gebieten geistigen Schaffens neue Kräfte wach geworden. Richard Strauss schrieb seine ersten sinfonischen Dichtungen, Hans Pfitzner begann mit der Musik zu Ibsens *Fest auf Solhaug* sein Lebenswerk, der junge Max Reger ließ aufhorchen. In Frankreich bestimmte Claude Debussy den Impressionismus; ein neuer Klangstil, beeinflußt durch wachsende Erkenntnisse exotischer Weisen und Skalen, begann sich zu entfalten. Gustav Mahler schuf seine ersten drei Sinfonien, und in Italien brachte der Verismo Mascagnis und Leoncavallos neue Tonfarben in das Opernschaffen, die bald in Puccini ihren vollendeten Höhepunkt fanden.

In diesen Jahren komponierte Anton Bruckner die 9. Sinfonie, sein nicht mehr zu Ende geführtes musikalisches Testament. Die Spanne von 1887 bis 1896 umgrenzt ihre Entstehung. Einem Wesen aus überirdischen Sphären gleichend, ragt sie in die so anders geartete Musik ihrer Umgebung, und man begreift nur zu gut, jetzt nach einem halben Jahrhundert, daß sie in ihrer Wucht, ihrem metaphysischen Grundton – widmete sie der Meister doch „dem lieben Gott" – nicht gleich und auch nicht in ihrem vollen Umfang verstanden wurde. Sie ist Anton Bruckners letztes, unvollendet gebliebenes Werk, seine „Summa musices", eine Vereinigung aller an des Meisters Schaffen zu beobachtenden sinfonischen Erscheinungen: der bis ins einzelne durchgebildeten Verarbeitungstechnik, seiner Gestaltung von Themengruppen und ihrer Zwischenglieder, der Einbeziehung kontrapunktischer Elemente, seiner Choralhöhepunkte wie seiner ungebrochenen Erfindungsgabe schlechthin. Das Finale sollte den Skizzen zufolge sowohl eine Fuge als auch einen weitgespannten Choral enthalten.

Like all of its predecessors, however, the Ninth Symphony is also a triumphant demonstration of Bruckner's absolute determination to forge a unity of form and content. The numerous surviving sketches provide illuminating examples not only of Bruckner's aims but of the steps that had to be taken in order before his ideas were translated into their final form. Anton Bruckner was not fortunate enough to be able to devote himself to composition unhindered. He continued to teach until 1894, though he was released from the task of giving lessons at the Conservatory in 1891 and of serving as organist at the Hofburgkapelle in 1892; in addition, deteriorating health increasingly impeded his creative work.

Research by Haas and Orel has established 21 September 1887 as the earliest known date at which Bruckner was engaged on the Ninth Symphony (first inscription of the opening, in score). He therefore probably began to conceive the symphony in the summer of 1887, presumably after completing the first copy of the score of the Eighth (on 9 August 1887). Further progress, however, was interrupted by other work. The revision of the Third Symphony (1888–89) was followed by that of the Eighth (1889–90); the Masses in E minor and F minor were revised again, in preparation for publication; and his receipt of an honorary doctorate from the University of Vienna led to a late revision of the First Symphony (1890–91). After going through the Second Symphony once more (1891–92), Bruckner then composed his setting of the 150th Psalm (in 1892) and the choral work *Helgoland* (in 1893). Although the draft of the Scherzo of the Ninth Symphony had been completed by 4 April 1889, and more concentrated attention was devoted to the symphony in 1891, it was not until *Helgoland* had been finished that Bruckner was able to commit himself to the symphony without interruption. From then onwards all of the strength that remained to him in his final years was dedicated to this task.

Die 9. Sinfonie ist aber auch wie alle ihre Vorgängerinnen ein überwältigendes Zeugnis von Bruckners unbedingtem Willen, der verlangte, daß Inhalt und Form sich vollkommen entsprechen. Die zahlreich erhalten gebliebenen Skizzen bieten aufschlußreiche Einzelheiten; aus ihnen werden nicht nur des Meisters Absichten, sondern auch der Weg, den sie zur endgültigen Gestalt zurücklegen mußten, sichtbar. Anton Bruckner hatte nicht das Glück, ungehemmt komponieren zu können. Noch bis 1894 gab er Unterricht, 1891 war er schon seiner Stunden am Konservatorium, 1892 seines Organistendienstes an der Hofburgkapelle entbunden worden; auch seine zunehmende Krankheit hinderte ihn mehr und mehr an seinem Schaffen.

Nach den bisherigen Forschungen von Haas und Orel ist das früheste feststellbare Kompositionsdatum für die 9. Sinfonie der 21. September 1887 (erste Partiturniederschrift des Anfangs). So erscheint es wahrscheinlich, daß Bruckner im Sommer 1887, vermutlich nach Beendigung der ersten Partiturniederschrift der 8. Sinfonie (9. August 1887), mit der Konzeption seiner „Neunten" begann. Die Weiterführung wurde aber vorerst noch durch andere Arbeiten zurückgedrängt: Der Umarbeitung der 3. Sinfonie (1888/1889) folgte die der 8. (1889/1890), die e-Moll- und f-Moll-Messe wurden zur Drucklegung noch einmal revidiert, das Ehrendoktorat der Universität Wien zog eine späte Umarbeitung der 1. Sinfonie (1890/1891) nach sich. Einer Durchsicht der 2. Sinfonie (1891/1892) reihte sich 1892 noch die Komposition des 150. Psalms und 1893 das Chorwerk *Helgoland* an. Wenn auch schon am 4. April 1889 das Scherzo entworfen und 1891 die Arbeit an der 9. Sinfonie intensiver fortgesetzt wurde, so war es Bruckner doch erst nach der Vollendung von *Helgoland* möglich, ohne Unterbrechung an diesem Werk zu arbeiten. Von da ab gehören alle Kräfte des schon alternden Meisters seiner 9. Sinfonie.

The autograph score, Bruckner's precious final bequest to posterity, is held in the Music Collection of the Österreichische Nationalbibliothek, shelf-mark ms.Hs. 19.481. The three completed movements it contains are dated as follows. The beginning of the first movement is marked 'Ende April $\overline{891}$.' and the end of the movement '14. 10. 92.' and '23. 12. 93'; the end of the Scherzo is marked '27. 2. $\overline{893}$.' and '15. 2. 94. Dr ABr.'; the end of the Adagio – and of the score as a whole – is marked '31. Okt. $\overline{894}$' and '30. Nov. $\overline{894}$. Wien. Dr A Bruckner.' This autograph forms the basis of Volume IX of the Complete Edition, published by Alfred Orel in 1934. For the present second edition, the text has been checked against the original once again and some misprints have been corrected. For technical reasons, however, the redundant accidentals in the first edition have been retained. Although this is not in conformance with modern engraving practice, it will perhaps be felt not to be inappropriate that Bruckner's distinctive style of notation should be reproduced in full in the case of at least one of his works. In the other volumes of the Complete Edition these 'warning' accidentals have been removed. All further details are dealt with in the Revisionsbericht, which will be supplemented in due course by a new edition of the 'Drafts and Sketches'.

The first performance of the Ninth Symphony was given in Vienna on 11 February 1903, seven years after Bruckner's death. Ferdinand Löwe, conducting the orchestra of the Wiener Konzertverein, undertook this courageous venture. As Auer reports, however, 'at each of the many rehearsals [he] zealously polished the score and altered the orchestration', with the result that the sound of the work was now very different from that which the composer had intended. Löwe acted from the best of motives; indeed, his efforts on behalf of Bruckner's entire œuvre remain as great as those of

So entstand Bruckners letzte Partitur. Sie ruht als kostbares Vermächtnis ihres Schöpfers in der Musiksammlung der Österreichischen Nationalbibliothek unter Signatur ms.Hs. 19.481. Die in ihr vereinigten drei vollendeten Sätze weisen folgende Datumseintragungen auf: Am Anfang des 1. Satzes: „Ende April $\overline{891}$.", an seinem Ende: „14. 10. 92." und „23. 12. 93"; am Ende des Scherzos: „27. 2. $\overline{893}$." und „15. 2. 94. Dr ABr."; am Ende des *Adagio* und damit der gesamten Partitur: „31. Okt. $\overline{894}$" und „30. Nov. $\overline{894}$. Wien. Dr A Bruckner." Dieses Autograph lag dem von Alfred Orel 1934 besorgten Band IX der Gesamtausgabe zugrunde. Die vorliegende 2. Ausgabe verglich den Druck neuerdings mit dem Original und verbesserte einige Stichfehler. Sie mußte allerdings aus technischen Gründen die in der 1. Ausgabe stehengebliebenen überflüssigen Versetzungszeichen beibehalten. Wenn damit auch den geltenden Stichregeln nicht entsprochen wird, so mag es dennoch nicht als abwegig empfunden werden, wenigstens an einem Werk Bruckners eigenartige Notierungsweise vollinhaltlich aufzuzeigen. Die anderen Bände der Gesamtausgabe haben diese „Vorsichts"-Versetzungszeichen Bruckners entfernt. Alle weiteren Einzelheiten enthält der Revisionsbericht, dem zu gegebenem Zeitpunkt auch die Neuauflage der „Entwürfe und Skizzen" folgen wird.

Die Uraufführung der 9. Sinfonie fand sieben Jahre nach des Meisters Tod am 11. Februar 1903 in Wien statt. Ferdinand Löwe wagte mit dem Wiener Konzertvereins-Orchester die Tat. Allerdings hatte er „in jeder der zahlreichen Proben eifrig gefeilt und instrumental geändert" (Auer), so daß das Werk ein anderes Klanggewand bekam, als sein Schöpfer ihm zugedacht hatte. Dies geschah in bester Absicht; die Verdienste Löwes um das Gesamtwerk Bruckners werden nach wie vor zu den größten zählen, die je ein Mensch um den Meister von St. Florian erworben hat. Als

any man. Nevertheless, when Siegmund von Hausegger, conducting the Munich Philharmonic Orchestra on 2 April 1932, gave an invited audience the opportunity of comparing the original with the work as it had hitherto been known, the symphony that Bruckner had actually envisaged came as a revelation. This was a Bruckner literally never heard before: it gave a glimpse into a new world. Since then, there has been a steady and irresistible change of attitude, culminating in the conviction of the vital importance of publishing the scores of Bruckner's works in the form in which he himself wrote them, free of all extraneous additions.

Leopold Nowak
Vienna, August 1951

A further careful check of the score of the Complete Edition has been made for the present Eulenburg edition. Special thanks are due to Rüdiger Bornhöft of Bremen for providing information on misprints and to Dr Walburga Litschauer of Vienna for her editorial collaboration.

For the Finale, Bruckner left numerous pages of score and short score as well as sketches. Without in any sense attempting to complete the movement, John A. Phillips of Adelaide, Australia has arranged these surviving sources in such as way as to provide a continuous musical sequence, which breaks off after 136 pages. This reconstruction, based entirely on Bruckner's autographs, was published by the Musikwissenschaftlicher Verlag of Vienna in 1994 as a supplementary volume to the Ninth Symphony.

Herbert Vogg
Vienna, 1994
Translation Richard Deveson

aber am 2. April 1932 Siegmund von Hausegger mit den Münchener Philharmonikern die bisher bekannte Klanggestalt des Werkes vor geladenen Gästen dem Original gegenüberstellte, da erkannte man erst, wie Bruckner selbst seine „Neunte" gewünscht hatte. Da offenbarte sich ein bis dahin nie gehörter Bruckner, öffneten sich die Blicke in neue Welten, strömten Anregungen hervor, die seither nicht mehr verstummt sind, sich verdichteten und in der Feststellung gipfelten, daß es unbedingt notwendig sei, die Partituren der Werke Bruckners nach seiner eigenen Handschrift, frei von allen Zutaten, zu veröffentlichen.

Leopold Nowak
Wien, August 1951

Für die Ausgabe in der Edition Eulenburg wurde die Partitur der Gesamtausgabe nochmals sorgfältig überprüft, wobei Herrn Rüdiger Bornhöft (Bremen) für die Mitteilung von Fehlern im Notentext und Frau Dr. Walburga Litschauer (Wien) für ihre redaktionelle Mitarbeit besonders zu danken ist.

Zum Finale hat Bruckner zahlreiche Partiturseiten, Particellseiten und Skizzen hinterlassen. John A. Phillips (Adelaide, Australien) hat die erhalten gebliebenen Quellen ohne jeden Ergänzungsversuch zu einem durchgehenden, nach 136 Seiten abbrechenden Satzverlauf geordnet. Diese einzig Bruckners Autographen berücksichtigende Rekonstruktion ist 1994 als Supplementband zur 9. Sinfonie im Musikwissenschaftlichen Verlag Wien erschienen.

Herbert Vogg
Wien, 1994

Orchestration/Orchesterbesetzung

Flöte 1–3
Oboe 1–3
Klarinette 1–3
Fagotte 1–3
Horn 1–8
Tenor-Tuba 1, 2
Baß-Tuba 3, 4
Trompete 1–3
Posaune 1–3
Kontra-Baßtuba
Pauken
Violine 1, 2
Viola
Violoncello
Kontrabaß

SYMPHONY No. 9

Anton Bruckner
(1824–1896)

I.

Edited by Leopold Nowak
© 1954 Musikwissenschaftlicher Verlag, Wien
Ernst Eulenburg Ltd

20
1.
Fl.
2.3.
1.
Ob.
2.3.
1.in B
Klar.
2.3.in B
1.
Fag.
2.3.
1.2.in F
3.4.in F
Hrn.
5.6.in F
7.8.in B
1.in F
Tromp.
2.3.in F
A.T.
Pos.
B.
K.-Btb.
Pk.
Viol.1
Viol.2
Vla.
Vc.
Kb.
cresc.
mf cresc.

A
40
1. Fl. 2.3.
1. Ob. 2.3.
1. in B Klar. 2.3. in B
1. Fag. 2.3.
1.2. in F 3.4. in F Hrn. 5.6. in F 7.8. in B
1. in F Tromp. 2.3. in F
A.T. Pos. B.
K.-Btb.
Pk.
Viol. 1
Viol. 2
Vla.
Vc.
Kb.
cresc. poco
cresc.
mf hervortretend

80
1. Fl. 2.3.
1. Ob. 2.3.
1. in B Klar. 2.3. in B
1. Fag. 2.3.
1.2. in F
3.4. in F
Hrn.
5.6. in F
7.8. in B
1. in F Tromp. 2.3. in F
A.T. Pos. B.
K.-Btb.
Pk.
Viol. 1
Viol. 2
Vla.
Vc.
Kb.
cresc.
pizz.

90

riten.
D
Langsamer
1. Fl. 2. 3.
1. Ob. 2. 3.
1. in B Klar. 2.3. in B
1. Fag. 2. 3.
1.2. in F
3.4. in F Hrn.
5.6. in F
7.8. in B
1. in F Tromp. 2.3. in F
A. T. Pos. B.
K.-Btb.
Pk.
Viol. 1
Viol. 2
Vla.
Vc.
Kb.
arco
pizz.
p gezogen

150
riten.
langsamer
1. Fl. 2. 3.
1. Ob. 2. 3.
1. in B Klar. 2. 3. in B
1. Fag. 2. 3.
1. 2. in F
3. 4. in F Hrn.
5. 6. in F
7. 8. in B
1. in F Tromp. 2. 3. in F
A. T. Pos. B.
K.-Btb.
Pk.
Viol. 1.
Viol. 2.
Vla.
Vc.
Kb.

24

200

1.
Fl.
2.3.
1.
Ob.
2.3.
1. in B
Klar.
2.3. in B
1.
Fag.
2.3.
1.2. in F
3.4. in F
Hrn.
5.6. in F
7.8. in B
mf cresc. sempre
1. in F
Tromp.
2.3. in F
A.T.
Pos.
B.
K.-Btb.
Pk.
Viol. 1
Viol. 2
Vla.
Vc.
Kb.

270
1.
Fl.
2.3.
1.
Ob.
2.3.
1. in B
Klar.
2.3. in B
1.
Fag.
2.3.
1.2. in F
3.4. in F
Hrn.
5.6. in F
7.8. in B
1. in F
Tromp.
2.3. in F
A.T.
Pos.
B.
K.-Btb.
Pk.
Viol. 1
Viol. 2
Vla.
Vc.
Kb.
dim.
divisi

310

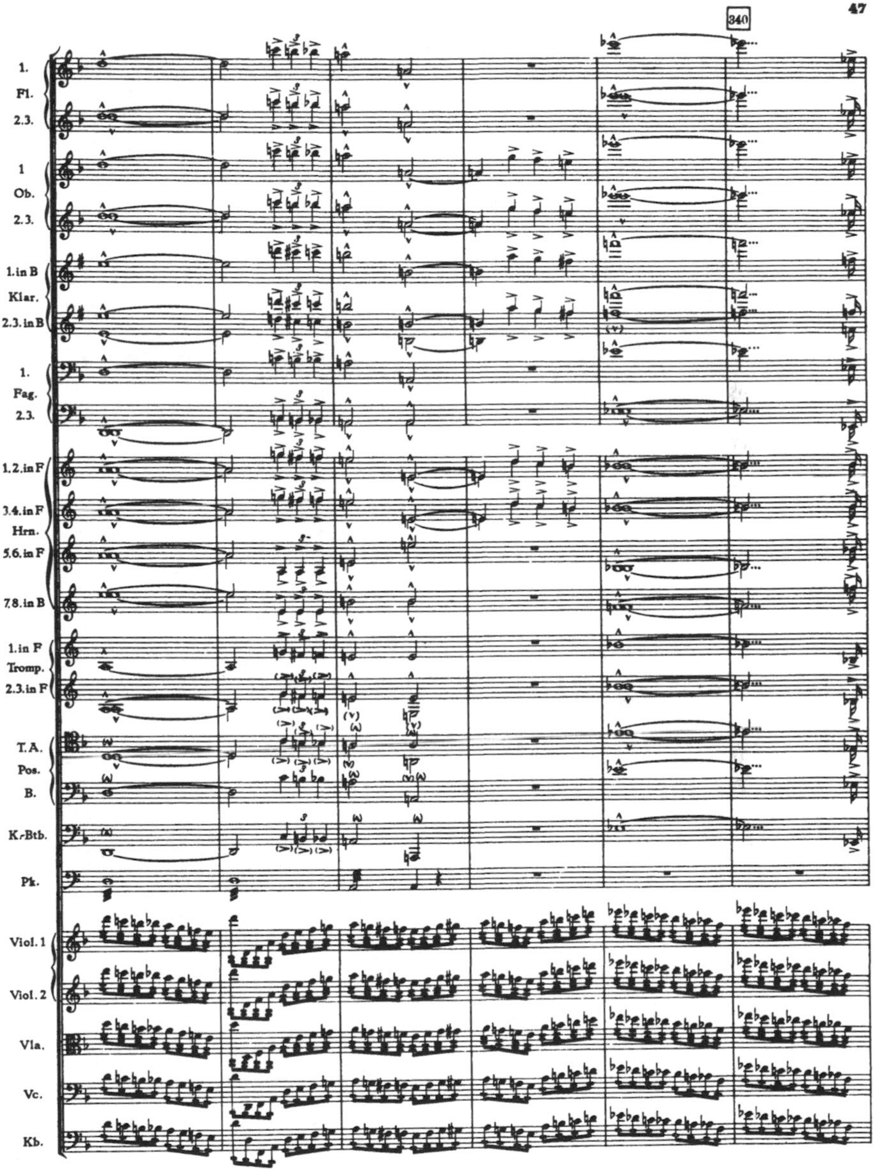
340
1.
Fl.
2.3.
1
Ob.
2.3.
1. in B
Klar.
2.3. in B
1.
Fag.
2.3.
1.2. in F
3.4. in F
Hrn.
5.6. in F
7.8. in B
1. in F
Tromp.
2.3. in F
T.A.
Pos.
B.
K.-Btb.
Pk.
Viol. 1
Viol. 2
Vla.
Vc.
Kb.

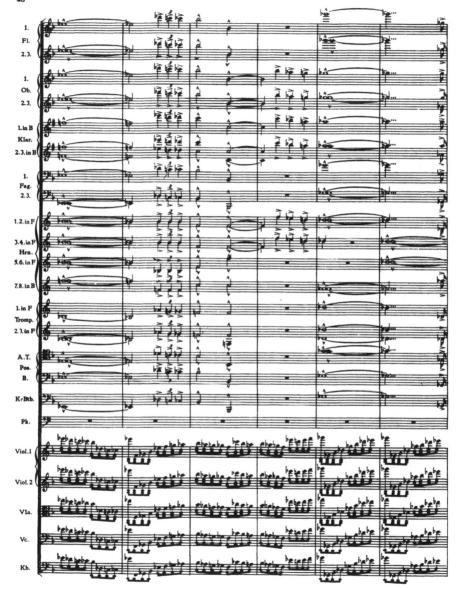

P
370
1.
Fl.
2.3.
1.
Ob.
2.3.
1. in B
Klar.
2.3. in B
1.
Fag.
2.3.
1.2. in F
3.4. in F
Hrn.
5.6. in F
7.8. in B
1. in F
Tromp.
2.3. in F
A.T.
Pos.
B.
K.-Btb.
Pk.
Viol. 1
Viol. 2
Vla.
Vc.
Kb.
gestopft
gestopft
offen
offen
p cresc.
p cresc.
mf (cresc.)
markiert gestrichen
markiert gestrichen
div.

380
1.
Fl.
2.3.
1.
Ob.
2.3.
1. in B
Klar.
2.3. in B
1.
Fag.
2.3.
1.2. in F
3.4. in F
Hrn.
5.6. in F
7.8. in F
7. u. 8. Horn in F
1. in F
Tromp.
2.3. in F
A.T.
Pos.
B.
K-Btb.
Pk.
Viol.1
Viol.2
Vla.
dim.
div.
Vc.
Kb.

a tempo

410
1.
Fl.
2. 3.
1.
Ob.
2. 3.
1. in B
Klar.
2.3. in B
1.
Fag.
2. 3.
1.2. in F
3.4. in F
Hrn.
5.6. in F
7.8. in B
1. in F
Tromp.
2.3. in F
A. T.
Pos.
B.
K.-Btb.
Pk.
Viol. 1
Viol. 2
Vla.
Vc.
Kb.

8 Langsamer

T
1. Fl. 2.3.
1. Ob. 2.3.
1. in B Klar. 2.3. in B
1. Fag. 2.3.
1.2. in F
3.4. in F
Hrn.
5.6. in F
7.8. in B
1. in F Tromp. 2.3. in F
A.T. Pos. B.
K.-Btb.
Pk.
Viol. 1
Viol. 2
Vla.
Vc.
Kb.
divisi

U Moderato 460

470

500

510

540
1.
Fl.
2.3.
1.
Ob.
2.3.
1. in B
Klar.
2.3. in B
1.
Fag.
2.3.
1.2. in F
3.4. in F
Hrn.
5.6. in F
7.8. in B
1. in F
Tromp.
2.3. in F
A.T.
Pos.
B.
K.-Btb.
Pk.
Viol. 1
Viol. 2
Vla.
Vc.
Kb.

II. Scherzo

20
1. Fl. 2.3.
1. Ob. 2.3.
1. in B Klar. 2.3. in B
1. Fag. 2.3.
1.2. in F
3.4. in F
Hrn.
5.6. in F
7.8. in B
1. in F Tromp. 2.3. in F
ppp
A.T. Pos. B.
K.-Btb.
Pk.
Viol. 1
mf
Viol. 2
p
Vla.
mf
Vc.
mf
Kb.

80
1.
Fl.
2.3.
1.
Ob.
2.3.
cresc. poco a poco
1. in B
Klar.
2.3. in B
cresc. poco a poco
cresc. poco a poco
mf
mf
1.
Fag.
2. 3.
1.2. in F
3.4. in F
Hrn.
5.6. in F
7.8. in B
1. in F
Tromp.
2.3. in F
cresc. poco a poco
A.T.
Pos.
B.
K.-Btb.
Pk.
Viol.1
cresc.
cresc.
f
Viol.2
cresc. poco a poco
mf
Vla.
cresc.
cresc.
Vc.
cresc.
cresc.
Kb.

40
1.
Fl.
2.3.
1.
Ob.
2.3.
1. in B
Klar.
2.3. in B
1.
Fag.
2.3.
1.2. in F
3.4. in F
Hrn.
5.6. in F
7.8. in B
1. in F
Tromp.
2.3. in F
A.T.
Pos.
B.
K.-Bth.
Pk.
Viol.1.
Viol.2.
Vla.
Vc.
Kb.
cresc.
f

A
50
1.
Fl.
2.3.
1.
Ob.
2.3.
1. in B
Klar.
2.3. in B
1.
Fag.
2.3.
1.2. in F
3.4. in F
Hrn.
5.6. in F
7.8. in B
1. in F
Tromp.
2.3. in F
A.T.
Pos.
B.
K.-Btb.
Pk.
trem.
Viol. 1
Viol. 2
Vla.
Vc.
Kb.
arco
ff

70
1. Fl. 2.3.
1. Ob. 2.3.
1. in B Klar. 2.3. in B
1. Fag. 2.3.
1.2. in F
3.4. in F Hrn.
5.6. in F
7.8. in B
1. in F Tromp. 2.3. in F
A.T. Pos. B.
K.-Btb.
Pk.
Viol. 1.
Viol. 2.
Vla.
Vc.
Kb.
pp
p
dim.

C
80
1. Fl. 2. 3.
1. Ob. 2. 3.
1. in B Klar. 2. 3. in B
1. Fag. 2. 3.
1. 2. in F
3. 4. in F
Hrn
5. 6. in F
7. 8. in B
1. in F Tromp. 2. 3. in F
A. T. Pos. B.
K.-Btb.
Pk.
Viol. 1
Viol. 2
Vla.
Vc.
Kb.
cresc. poco a poco
cresc.
mf
p

allmählich bewegter

150
1.
Fl.
2.3.
1
Ob.
2.3.
pp
1. in B
Klar.
2.3. in B
1.
Fag.
2.3.
1.2. in F
ppp
3.4. in F
Hrn.
5.6. in F
7.8. in B
1. in F
Tromp.
2.3. in F
ppp
A.T.
Pos.
B.
K.-Btb.
Pk.
spicc. sempre
Viol.1
pp
arco
spicc. sempre
Viol.2
pp
Vla.
Vc.
Kb.

160
G
a tempo
1.
Fl.
2.3.
1.
Ob.
2.3.
1. in B
Klar.
2.3. in B
1.
Fag.
2.3.
1.2. in F
3.4. in F
Hrn.
5.6. in F
7.8. in B
1. in F
Tromp.
2.3. in F
A.T.
Pos.
B.
K.-Btb.
Pk.
Viol. 1
Viol. 2
Vla.
Vc.
Kb.
arco
arco
arco

190
1.
Fl.
2.3.
1.
Ob.
2.3.
1. in B
Klar.
2.3. in B
1.
Fag
2.3.
1.2. in F
3.4. in F
Hrn.
5.6. in F
7.8. in B
1. in F
Tromp.
2.3. in F
A.T.
Pos.
B.
K.-Btb.
Pk.
Viol. 1
Viol. 2
Vla.
Vc.
Kb.
p
pp
(dim.)
dim.

210
1. Fl. 2.3.
1. Ob. 2.3.
1. in B Klar. 2.3. in B
1. Fag. 2.3.
1.2. in F
3.4. in F Hrn.
5.6. in F
7.8. in B
1. in F Tromp. 2.3. in F
A.T. Pos. B.
K.-Btb.
Pk.
Viol. 1
Viol. 2
Vla.
Vc.
Kb.

220
L
1.
Fl.
2.3.
1.
Ob.
2.3.
1. in B
Klar.
2.3. in B
1.
Fag.
2.3.
1.2. in F
3.4. in F
Hrn.
5.6. in F
7.8. in B
1. in F
Tromp.
2.3. in F
A.T.
Pos.
B.
K.-Btb.
Pk.
Viol. 1
Viol. 2
Vla.
Vc.
Kb.
ff
p
gestrichen

280
1.
Fl.
2.3
1.
Ob.
2.3.
1. in B
Klar.
2.3. in B
1.
Fag.
2.3.
ff marc. sempre
ff marc. sempre
1.2. in F
3.4. in F
Hrn.
5.6. in F
7.8. in B
1. in F
Tromp.
2.3. in F
A.T.
Pos.
B.
K.-Btb.
Pk.
Viol. 1
Viol. 2
Vla.
Vc.
Kb.
ff

Trio

Schnell

20
1. Fl.
2. 3.
1. Ob.
2. 3.
1. in B Klar.
2.3. in B
1. Fag.
2. 3.
1. 2. in F
3.4. in F Hrn.
5.6. in F
7.8. in B
1. in F Tromp.
2.3. in F
A. T. Pos.
B.
K.-Btb
Pk.
Viol. 1
Viol. 2
Vla.
Vc.
Kb.
mf
dim. sempre
p
hervortretend

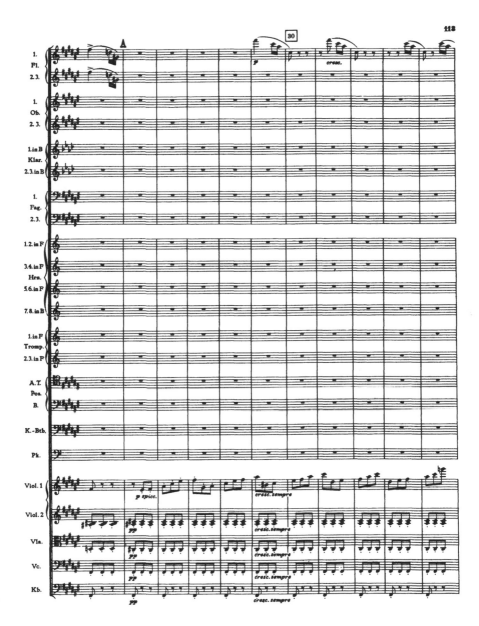

50
B
1.
Fl.
2.3.
1.
Ob.
2.3.
1.in B
Klar.
2.3.in B
1.
Fag.
2.3.
1.2.in F
3.4.in F
Hrn.
5.6.in F
7.8.in B
1.in F
Tromp.
2.3.in F
A.T.
Pos.
B.
K.-Btb.
Pk.
Viol.1
Viol.2
Vla.
Vc.
Kb.
cresc.
dim.
arco

90
1.
Fl.
2.3.
1.
Ob.
2.3.
1.in B
Klar.
2.3.in B
1.
Fag.
2.3.
1.2.in F
3.4.in F
Hrn.
5.6.in F
7.8.in B
1.in F
Tromp.
2.3.in F
A.T.
Pos.
B.
K.-Btb.
Pk.
Viol.1
Viol.2
Vla.
Vc.
Kb.

E Langsamer 140

150
F a tempo
160
1.
Fl.
2.3.
1.
Ob.
2.3.
1.in B
Klar.
2.3.in B
1.
Fag.
2.3.
1.2.in F
3.4.in F
Hrn.
5.6.in F
7.8.in B
1.in F
Tromp.
2.3.in F
A.T.
Pos.
B.
Kr.Btb.
Pk.
Viol.1
Viol.2
Vla.
Vc.
Kb.
arco
p spicc.
pizz.

170
1.
Fl.
2. 3.
1.
Ob.
2. 3.
1. in B
Klar.
2. 3. in B
1.
Fag.
2. 3.
1. 2. in F
3. 4. in F
Hrn.
5. 6 in F
7. 8. in B
1. in F
Tromp.
2. 3. in F
A. T.
Pos.
B.
K.-Btb.
Pk.
Viol. 1
Viol. 2
Vla.
Vc.
Kb.
p
mf
hervortretend
cresc. sempre

J
230
240
1. Fl. 2.3.
1. Ob. 2.3.
1. in B Klar. 2.3. in B
1. Fag. 2.3.
1.2. in F 3.4. in F Hrn. 5.6. in F 7.8. in B
1. in F Tromp. 2.3. in F
A.T. Pos. B.
K.-Btb.
Pk.
Viol. 1
Viol. 2
Vla.
Vc.
Kb.
arco
pp spicc.
pizz.
pizz.
pizz.
pizz.

250

260

Scherzo da Capo

III. Adagio

70
1. Fl. 2. 3.
1. Ob. 2. 3.
1. in B Klar. 2. 3. in B
1. Fag. 2. 3.
1. 2. in F Hrn. 3. 4. in F
Ten.-Tb. 1. 2. in B
B.-Tb. 1. 2. in F
1. in F Tromp. 2. 3. in F
A. T. Pos. B.
K.-Btb.
Pk.
Viol. 1
Viol. 2
Vla.
Vc.
Kb.
p
mf
dim.

Tempo wie im Anfange   80

120
H
1. Fl. 2. 3.
1. Ob. 2. 3.
1. in B Klar. 2. 3. in B
1. Fag. 2. 3.
1. 2. in F Hrn. 3. 4. in F
Ten.-Tb. 1. 2 in B
B.-Tb. 1. 2. in F
1. in F Tromp. 2. 3. in F
A. T. Pos. B.
K-Btb.
Pk.
Viol. 1a
Viol. 1b
Viol. 2
Vla.
Vc.
Kb.
cresc. sempre
cresc. sempre

140
K
1.
Fl.
2.3.
1.
Ob.
2.3.
1. in B
Klar.
2.3. in B
in A
in A
1.
Fag.
2.3.
1.2. in F
Hrn.
3.4. in F
Ten.-Tb.
1.2. in B
B.-Tb.
1.2. in F
1. in F
Tromp.
2.3. in F
A.T.
Pos.
B.
K.-Btb.
Pk.
Viol. 1
Viol. 2
Vla.
Vc.
Kb.
f
f
cresc.
markig
breit

1.
Fl.
2.3.
1.
Ob.
2.3.
1. in A
Klar.
2.3. in A
1.
Fag.
2.3.
1.2. in F
Hrn.
3.4. in F
Ten.-Tb.
1.2. in B
B.-Tb.
1.2. in F
1. in F
Tromp.
2.3. in F
A.T.
Pos.
B.
K.-Btb.
Pk.
Viol. 1
Viol. 2
Vla.
Vc.
Kb.
f
ff
cresc.
ff marc.
(arco)

150
1.
Fl.
2. 3.
1.
Ob.
2. 3.
1. in A
Klar.
2. 3. in A
1.
Fag.
2. 3.
1. 2. in F
Hrn.
3. 4. in F
Ten.-Tb.
1. 2. in B
B.-Tb.
1. 2. in F
1. in F
Tromp.
2. 3. in F
A. T.
Pos.
B.
K.-Btb.
Pk.
Viol. 1
Viol. 2
Vla.
Vc.
Kb.
pp

160

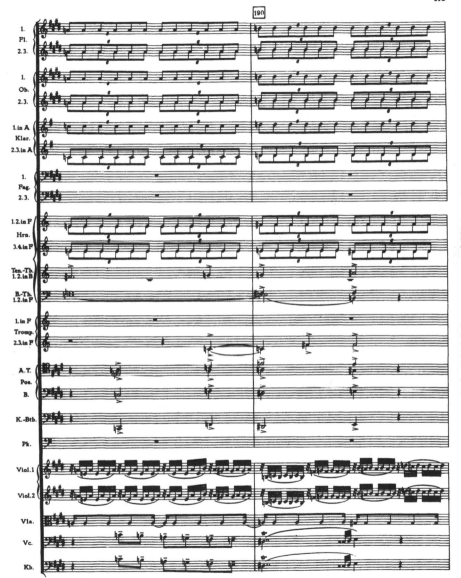

177

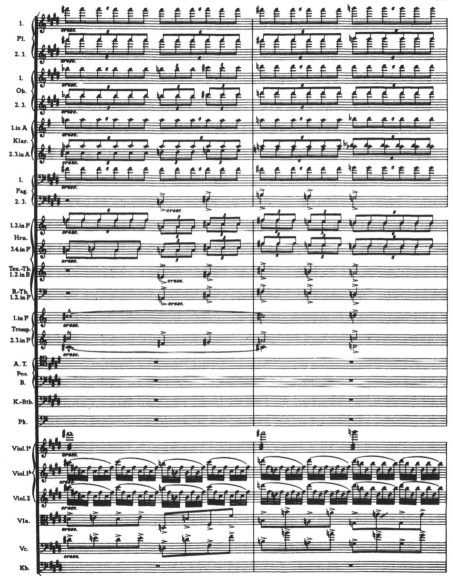

210
S
1.
Fl.
2.3.
1.
Ob.
2.3.
1. in A
Klar.
2.3. in A
1.
Fag.
2.3.
1.2. in F
Hrn.
3.4. in F
Ten.-Tb.
1.2. in B
B.-Tb.
1.2. in F
1. in F
Tromp.
2.3. in F
A.T.
Pos.
B.
K.-Btb.
Pk.
Viol. 1
Viol. 2
Vla.
Vc.
Kb.
p marc.
cresc.
(cresc.)

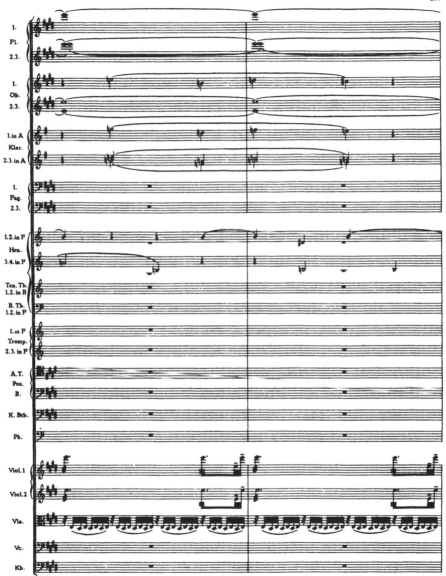

W
1.
Fl.
2.3.
1.
Ob.
2.3.
1.in A
Klar.
2.3.in A
1.
Fag.
2.3.
1.2.in F
Hrn.
3.4.in F
Ten.-Tb.
1.2.in B
B.-Tb.
1.2.in F
1.in F
Tromp.
2.3.in F
A.T.
Pos.
B.
K.-Btb.
Pk.
Viol.1
Viol.2
Vla.
Vc.
Kb.